A Fresh Start

Burnout & Recovery in Ministry

Marc Brûlé

COPYRIGHT

A Fresh Start

Burnout and Recovery in Ministry

Published by Capstone Press

Welland, ON

Canada

capstonepress@gmail.com

Copyright © 2020 by Capstone Press

Unless otherwise noted, all Scripture quotations are taken from the Holy Bible, New International Version®, NIV®. Copyright © 1973, 1978, 1984, 2011 by Biblica, Inc.™ Used by permission of Zondervan. All rights reserved worldwide. www.zondervan.com The "NIV" and "New International Version" are trademarks registered in the United States Patent and Trademark Office by Biblica, Inc.™

Scripture quotations marked NLT are taken from the Holy Bible, New Living Translation, copyright © 1996, 2004, 2015 by Tyndale House Foundation. Used by permission of Tyndale House Publishers, Inc., Carol Stream, Illinois 60188. All rights reserved.

Scriptures marked ESV are taken from The ESV® Bible (The Holy Bible, English Standard Version®). ESV® Text Edition: 2016. Copyright © 2001 by Crossway, a publishing ministry of Good News Publishers. The ESV® text has been reproduced in cooperation with and by permission of Good News Publishers. Unauthorized reproduction of this publication is prohibited. All rights reserved.

All Rights Reserved. This book, or any portion thereof, may not be reproduced or transmitted in any form or by any means, electronic or mechanical, including photocopying, recording, or by an information storage and retrieval system (except by a reviewer, who may quote brief passages in a review or other endorsement, or in a recommendation to be printed in a magazine, newspaper, or on the Internet) without written permission from the publisher.

ISBN: 978-1-7770485-1-8

Table Of Contents

Burnout Happens	1
Signs of Burnout	13
Burnout Recovery	21
Burnout Prevention	65
New Beginnings	77

FOREWORD

Let me begin by saying I am a strong believer in what Jesus said when he declared "I will build my church and the gates of hell shall not prevail against it." (Matt 16:18, ESV) Jesus is the source and the completion of his Church. He designed her. He will complete her.

What I sometimes question is not Jesus' promise to build His church, but whether what we are building is like what he designed and intended. When the statistics point to an alarming amount of pastors leaving the ministry every month in the United States, I question the design and function of our present church systems. This is not something I'm trying to fix in this book. That task is far beyond its reaches. What I am endeavouring to accomplish is to equip pastors and church leaders to achieve a healthy, sustainable pastoral ministry within the church.

Pastoral ministry has become a precarious vocation. Pastors, their spouses, and their children all face challenges that I don't believe were ever God's intention. I believe it is the heart of God that pastors and their families be spiritually, emotionally, and physically healthy in order to fulfil his call on their lives. Healthy pastors foster healthy churches. Healthy churches grow healthy communities.

This is the goal of this book—to build healthy pastors, healthy churches, healthy communities.

There are numerous books available that cover burnout in depth. Since I am not an expert in this field, my goal in writing this book is to share my life story and some helpful principles in a short format that will be helpful to leaders—

pastors, ministry leaders, boards and elders. This is intended to equip all of us to work together for health.

PREFACE

Letter to Church Leadership Teams

One of the inspirations for writing this book comes from a request by fellow pastors and ministers to have something on the topic of burnout available for their boards, elders, and leadership teams. If you fall into one of these categories, this book will provide insight into what your pastor may experience in his role. As part of the core leadership you hold an important role in the health of the church and the pastor. Sometimes you may feel like you are caught in a tension between the two. Whether you feel the tension or not, the information provided here may help to equip you with a greater understanding and a better perspective and will likely bring wisdom into your leadership role.

Churches and ministries have various leadership models ranging from congregational rule to a somewhat autocratic model. This book is not a discussion on the merits of governance models, but rather a communication of vital information about maintaining healthy relationships between the pastor, the leadership core, and the congregation regardless of the system you use.

The ultimate goal is fruitful ministry for all involved and healthy, godly lifestyles to support that design. Please read this information with an open heart, perhaps seeing your pastor and his family in a new light.

ACKNOWLEDGEMENTS

There are several people I would like to thank—those who supported me in the writing of this book and those who have journeyed with me and supported me during my recovery and restoration.

For the Book

I want to thank the pastors and ministry leaders in the city of Welland who advised and inspired me to write about my burnout with leaders and boards in mind. I hope this blesses and helps each of you in your own ministries.

Thanks to Lorraine Cheshire for helping with editing and content. Your encouragement gave me the extra boost I needed.

Thank you Rachel Thomson for giving me some key insight and direction for writing. I appreciate your expertise and enthusiasm.

For the Journey

Thank you to the elders of WellSpring Community Church who supported and shielded me during the most difficult time of my life. Thank you for seeing past the mess of the moment and believing in God's restorative work.

Thank you to Andrew Thompson for stepping up as interim pastor during my time off. What a witness of God's great grace! You have been such a blessing to me; you will never really know the depth of what you have given me. And thanks for working with me to make adjustments so we can continue to work together as associates.

Thanks to the staff and volunteers of WellSpring for stepping up during a trying time. Once again, God's faithfulness was displayed through yours.

Thanks to the congregation of WellSpring. It was a dark and confusing time for many, yet so many of you stayed the course, stepped up, and saw it through. We are all healthier because of it.

Thank you to Joan Hyatt, my Christian therapist, who played such a vital role in my recovery. You saw for me what I could no longer see. You hold a place of deep esteem and appreciation in my heart.

Thanks to David McGrew who covered me and gave me the space I needed. You protected me from judgment and shame. I want to be like you when I grow up!

To my children, Amy, Jonathan, and Adam who didn't always know how to respond or behave around me during my lowest points, thank you! I knew your hearts were filled with love and care for me.

To my wife, Wendy, thank you for not giving up. You responded in ways beyond my expectation which alleviated my apprehension. I was often overwhelmed by the depth of love you showed me. You modelled what I'd like to be. Your acceptance, your patience, your encouragement, and your determination continue to bring tears to my eyes whenever I think of you in those days. I love you dearly!

To my Lord, Jesus Christ, you truly are good! You helped me learn once again, "Jesus loves me! This I know, for the Bible tells me so." Thank you for your patience and faithfulness. Thank you for your call on my life. But most importantly, thank you that I am your son.

CHAPTER ONE
Burnout Happens

Stop!

Many of us are in the habit of skipping the foreword and preface of a book and jumping right into the chapters. I ask you to take the extra few minutes to go back and read the forward and preface before you dig into the rest of the book. They are short but important. They are key to framing the rest of the content of this book.

My Story

It was a monthly Sunday evening Encounter service. I was in my office beforehand, and suddenly I felt my heart pounding. I felt something was very wrong. All that was going through my mind was, I can't go out there and have anyone need me. I was shaking. I wondered if I was going to have a heart attack. It was a terrifying moment. It was my first ever panic attack. I took a few minutes to get myself together and finally, did go out into the service. I did survive. I went home feeling quite upset about what had taken place. I was afraid—for myself—about the future. Could I keep going on like this? And so began a long process toward wholeness.

I sensed a call to ministry at the age of six. Even in my turbulent teens, as I wrestled with temptation and played both sides of the fence, I still knew deep down in my heart that I was called to full-time ministry.

By age twenty three, I had become the senior pastor of a struggling church. We, as a church, worked through the struggles, grew, got out of debt, and flourished. It was not without its challenges but was well worth every bit of heart and investment.

When I first recognized burnout in my life, I had pastored that same church for almost twenty-nine years. During those years I had also led the city ministerial for fifteen years, been the national worship leader for Promise Keepers Canada, sat on the boards of two national ministries, and provided some mentoring and support to other pastors. Married for thirty years with three children that loved and served God (and still do), I considered myself blessed from pretty well every angle.

However, some long-term subtle stresses and unhealthy practices in my life were slowly creeping in and invading my personal world. Some seemed quite benign. Nighttime snacking while watching Netflix hardly seemed harmful, yet the drive behind the behaviour was where the problem really lay. I was escaping by numbing and self-medicating with food and entertainment. Neither are inherently evil. This is why burnout can be so deceiving; it can mask itself in seemingly neutral behaviours.

It all came to a point of crisis in April, 2015. By then, I was watching four to five hours of Netflix television series a day both at the office and at home. My productivity dropped significantly, yet I could still prep and preach well, counsel others, cover the basics of administration, envision and work toward the church's future, and generally, do well at family life. Then, seemingly suddenly, I felt my life spin out of control. I faced temptations that overwhelmed me and tormented my mind. I ate snack foods uncontrollably. I watched, and watched, and watched TV programs and movies. In all of this, I experienced guilt and shame, yet that drove me more into unhealthy coping strategies. Then it hit me at the church on that Sunday evening I described.

On Tuesday, two days later, as I was preparing for our office staff meeting, I was experiencing something totally different. I was not fearful, I was cold—very cold. I had the thermostat set at 24°C (75°F) which is quite warm in the Canadian spring weather, yet I was wearing a jacket zipped up to the neck and was still shivering. When I walked into the main office and asked if anyone was cold, the answer was a clear no.

Now I knew something was significantly wrong. Not only was I out of control, but my body was showing significant signs of stress. I made an appointment with a Christian therapist. My opening statement to her was, "I feel like I'm slipping off a tin roof and have nothing to grab on to." And so began the long journey toward restoration and health.

The process was arduous—for me, for my family, and for the church. However, the growth and health that resulted from it are a testimony to God's faithfulness.

What is Burnout?

Burnout is a form of accumulated exhaustion. *The Merriam Webster Dictionary Online* states in the definition of burnout that it usually results from "prolonged stress or frustration." Other professionals suggest that it can result from settings that are emotionally taxing. Burnout is physical, emotional, mental, and spiritual exhaustion as the result of excessive and prolonged stress.

Stress is not necessarily bad. Good stress occurs when we have happy events like a wedding; it keeps us feeling excited about life. Common everyday stressors can also be good for us as they motivate us to work and to accomplish our goals. On the other hand, stress can become problematic when stress levels stay activated for long periods of time—chronic stress.

Stress activates a physiological response. Adrenaline is one of the hormones released in the body to help us deal with stress; it gives us the ability to swerve our vehicle quickly to avoid an accident. It also causes our heart to pound. I am certain we have all experienced this. You may have heard of the fight-flight-freeze response. It is our brain's response to crisis. Again, this is a blessing to us when there is a threat or danger. However, we are not designed to continually experience this state. Our bodies need recovery time. Burnout happens when the stress levels are too high over an extended period.

Depending on church size, roles and responsibilities, pastors must use their energy in significant and various ways. They need mental energy for planning, sermon preparation, vision development, administration, etc. They need emotional energy for supporting parishioners and staff, in addition to their spouse and family. They need social energy for interacting with people in small and larger settings—this can be extremely taxing especially for an introvert. They need physical energy to do all of the above and often work late into the night. Meanwhile, their job is primarily sedentary—sit, study, read, pray, sit, talk, listen, sit, sit, sit. As a result, they have a tendency to be less physically fit, resulting in reduced stamina and resilience. They also need spiritual energy as this job is predominantly spiritual in nature. Eternal souls are at stake. Pastors are engaged in a spiritual battle.

All of these forms of energy consumption combined, without proper care, can slowly deplete a pastor's tank until there is nothing left—this is exhaustion, burnout.

Another factor that contributes to burnout is the need to perform tasks that are not in the pastor's gifting or skill set. Using our skills and gifts energizes us even though we may be tired at the end of the day. On the other hand, working in areas where we do not possess the skills or gifts, drains and frustrates us along with making us feel tired. We all need to do things outside our skill set, and that's fine if it is only 20 percent of our workload while the remaining 80 percent is what we do well. Unfortunately, many a pastor spends much more than 20 percent of his time on things that are not his strengths. This drains more energy, more quickly.

Your age can also play a part in your susceptibility to burnout. You cannot do in your fifties what you were able to power through in your thirties. If you don't make adjustments for age and stage changes, you will set yourself up to fail. It is not failure to adjust to your stage of life. It is wisdom.

Burnout and clinical depression are not the same, but the factors that lead to burnout can also contribute to clinical depression. When the pastor suffers with both conditions, it places him, his family, and his church at a higher risk than just having burnout alone. Combined, they can lead to significant moral failure and personal compromise of core values. There are times when medical treatment is necessary from the resulting depression, though not always.

Burnout Happens

Burnout happens. Nobody plans on it. No pastor makes a career decision to burnout and become depressed, jeopardizing his ministry, marriage, family, and future. But it happens.

Ministry leaders, especially pastors, give their hearts to caring. They care for the lost. They care for the weak.

They care for their families. They care for their churches. They carry a sense of responsibility in their hearts that others generally don't understand or appreciate.

Pastoring is a role that doesn't allow you to leave work at the office. You are thinking about people. You are thinking about Sunday's message. You are thinking about money. All of this is often processed alone or at least internalized.

Then there is the challenge of expectations. There are spoken and unspoken ones. There are realistic and unrealistic ones. Who gets to sort them out and decide where the boundaries should be?

Church goers often carry with them specific sets of expectations. These vary based on upbringing, experience, assumptions, and even culture. Should the pastor visit every member throughout the year? Should the pastor visit the sick regularly? Should the pastor be on call even on his day off? Should the pastor do the administrative work? Should the pastor—? You get the point. On top of that, there are internal expectations that any pastor places on himself. Are there unrealistic expectations? Is there a fear of failure?

The ambiguities, the care, and the expectations can all contribute to burnout. So the question arises: Is burnout preventable? Yes! Can it be recovered from? Yes! This is why I have written this short book. Hopefully it will serve as a template for avoiding, recognizing, and recovering from burnout.

God wants pastors and churches to be healthy. Healthy pastors produce healthy churches. Unhealthy pastors produce unhealthy churches. Whether you are a pastor or part of a church leadership team (board member, elder, etc.), you play a key role in fostering a healthy church.

The Need for Self-Care

Keep a close watch on yourself and on the teaching. Persist in this, for by so doing you will save both yourself and your hearers. (1 Timothy 4:16, ESV)

Keep a close watch on how you live and on your teaching. Stay true to what is right for the sake of your own salvation and the salvation of those who hear you. (1 Timothy 4:16, NLT)

Remember your leaders, who spoke the word of God to you. Consider the outcome of their way of life and imitate their faith. (Hebrews 13:7)

It is vital that a pastor prioritizes his own personal life and spirituality as of first importance. Yet this is one of the easiest things for a pastor to lose sight and control of. Pastors generally spend their time focused on others' needs—spiritual, emotional, relational, physical, and so on. Consequently, it becomes easy for a pastor to spend all of his prayer and devotional time focused on what God wants to do in others. He does this at his own expense. Every time he reads his Bible, he looks for what will fit in a sermon or what will help someone he recently met with. He becomes more of a spiritual food processor than the eater of the food.

God has called all of us to be life-givers out of overflow. The Bible speaks of cups that overflow and rivers that flow and spill over with life. But pastors can become pipelines for living water rather than overflowing containers of water. Ministry happens. People's needs are met. Sadly, the pastor is slowly drying and dying as the water is not reaching his own heart. He must take care of his own life so he can serve out of overflow.

Proper self-care consists of rest, nurture, and investment—physical, emotional, mental, and spiritual. It is about knowing how to establish life balance. He must also have sufficient time off to disengage from the pressures of ministry and truly rest to be refreshed. Vacations **and** sabbaticals both play a role in the pastor's health.

The overflow of that kind of health will result in greater spiritual authority and increased credibility as he models a life worth emulating.

Facing the Facts

I have gathered some statistics to show how significantly stress affects pastors. These are American statistics; however, given the similarity of church culture between the United States and Canada, I believe these stats would also be relevant for Canadians.

According to an article in the *New York Times* (August 1, 2010), public health experts found that "members of the clergy now suffer from obesity, hypertension, and depression at rates higher than most Americans." They go on to say that "in the last decade, their use of antidepressants has risen, while their life expectancy has fallen." They also found that many clergy wished they could change professions. More recent statistics reported by PastoralCareInc.com (2018) shed more light on the status of the matter:

- 84% of pastors feel they are on call 24/7.
- **80%** believe pastoral ministry has **negatively** affected their families. Many pastor's [*sic*] children do not attend church now because of what the church has done to their parents.
- 78% of pastors report having their vacation and personal time interrupted with ministry duties or expectations.
- 57% of pastors believe they do not receive a livable wage.
- **75%** of pastors report significant **stress-related** crisis [*sic*] at least once in their ministry.
- **80%** of pastors and **84%** of their spouses have felt unqualified and discouraged as role of pastors at least one or more times in their ministry.
- **52%** of pastors feel overworked and cannot meet their church's unrealistic expectations.
- **70%** of pastors report they have a **lower self-image now** than when they first started.
- 84% of pastors desire to have close fellowship with someone they can trust and confide in.
- Over 50% of pastors are unhealthy, overweight, and do not exercise.
- 71% of churches have no plan for a pastor to receive a periodic sabbatical.

- 30% of churches have no documentation clearly outlining what the church expects of their pastor.
- **1** out of every **10** pastors will actually retire as a pastor. [1]

These stats should serve as a wakeup call to pastors and church leadership teams (boards, elders, deacons, etc.). They clearly indicate that we, in the church world, have created a form of ministry that is not part of God's design. We need to find a way back to what God intended for pastoral ministry and church community. This begins by addressing the immediate problem—burnout and what contributes to it.

On the other hand, there is some good news.

- 73% of churches are treating their pastors better. This statistic has improved due to the advent of clergy appreciation, better education on the role of the pastor, and denominational awareness to better supporting their pastors.
- 77% of pastors, especially millennials (younger pastors ages usually born around 1978-1990), are spending 20 or more hours with their families each week.
- 90% of pastors feel they are called and in the place where God has called them. [2]

---

[1] "Statistics in the Ministry" Pastoral Care Inc., 2018, https://www.pastoralcareinc.com/statistics/
[2] Ibid.

This is a clear sign that people are becoming more aware of the need for healthy pastors and healthy churches.

CHAPTER TWO
Signs of Burnout

Burnout

It doesn't happen all at once, yet it feels like it happens all of a sudden. The progression toward burnout is subtle; it is easily missed and masked. Burnout does not look the same for everyone, yet there are common traits and signs. However, different personalities will have different experiences and will display different behaviours.

Many of the symptoms of burnout appear to be relatively harmless, but when the tipping point is reached, they can be devastating—to the person, to the marriage, to the family, and to the church.

Burnout is primarily the result of chronic stress, as we covered in Chapter 1. Stress can intensify when the pastor has to spend significant amounts of energy on activities that are not his strengths. Stress also comes as a result of ongoing crisis management, unhealthy relationships with leadership or church members, ongoing criticism or disapproval from leadership or church members, and the pastor's disappointment in himself.

The signs of burnout listed below are not exhaustive; they are among the most commonly agreed upon. Keep in mind that symptoms exist on a continuum. They also appear in the five vital aspects of a person's life: spiritual, mental/emotional, physical, relational, and behavioural.

Spiritual Symptoms

- Prolonged spiritual dryness: We all go through desert times in our spiritual lives. Burnout can lead to prolonged seasons of dryness. There is a loss of desire for prayer, devotional time, and study of Scripture.
- Depersonalized spiritual life: You stop reading the Bible for yourself. Every passage is simply a resource for another sermon or someone else's situation. The Bible is no longer personal spiritual food. It is reduced to a tool of the trade.
- Prayerlessness: Prayer mostly becomes about what is needed in ministry: praying with others and praying in church services. Very little prayer is communion with God. Prayer becomes laborious—it can also be a consistently joyless experience.

Mental/Emotional Symptoms

- Lack of mental energy: You have no drive. You feel like you are getting nowhere.

- Low morale: You feel like a failure much of the time.
- Reduced coping ability: You cannot handle stress or challenges you normally could.
- Depletion: You feel mentally and emotionally empty.
- Lack of motivation: Work is a dread. You would rather avoid work most of the time.

Physical Symptoms

- Significant weight gain or loss: You lose your appetite, or lose control of it. Eating becomes a coping mechanism.
- Muscle tension and headaches: Loss of motivation often includes reduced physical activity which contributes to the muscle tension.
- Others ailments: Other ailments, such as gastrointestinal problems, hypertension, and ulcers can be induced or intensified.

Relational Symptoms

- Increased conflict in family: You are less patient with others and are more easily irritated.
- Withdrawal from relationships: You tend to isolate yourself to avoid relational tension.
- Increased negative attitude: Generally this is directed toward people.
- Changes in sexual desire: Your sexual desire decreases or your libido becomes low.

- Codependency: You define yourself by your relationships with others or, most significantly, your ministry. You don't know who you are aside from your ministry. Your inability to say no to people's needs is a primary indicator of this.

Behavioural Symptoms

- Escapist behaviour: This is where you develop coping mechanisms to escape the pain and sense of failure or despair. The specific behaviours range from the fairly benign (e.g., excessive TV/movie time, obsessive sports/hobbies, extended isolation, internet escapism) to the dangerous (e.g., drugs, alcohol, pornography, sexual encounters).
- Decreased productivity: Productivity drops by a significant amount. Phone calls are not returned. Emails are not responded to. Office work is not completed. Sermon prep is last minute. The quality and quantity of work decreases significantly. Your creativity also greatly diminishes.

These are just some of the symptoms of burnout. Someone may have a few of these and still not be burned out. It can, however, be a sign post that burnout is just around the corner. The greater the number of symptoms, or the greater the intensity of the symptoms, the higher the likelihood the pastor is in burnout.

Depression

Depression can accompany burnout. Depression can contribute to burnout. Burnout can contribute to depression. The issue is not what comes first, but that both be recognized and dealt with.

Clinical depression still carries a degree of taboo in much of the church world. There is a general lack of knowledge and understanding when it comes to psychological and mental disorders. We must consider that there can be physical, psychological, and spiritual factors in depression. Ignoring one of these will not rectify the others. We must take care not to be quick to judge someone as they face depression.

This taboo can easily carry over to pastors. We place unhealthy expectations on ourselves. I just need to pray more, trust God more, read my Bible more, etc. We end up tormenting ourselves because we are not "overcoming" our persistent sadness which reinforces the symptoms of depression all the more.

Clinical depression is defined as a mood disorder caused by various factors such as genetic predisposition, stress, and brain chemistry. Extended periods of stress can alter brain chemistry bringing depression into play. The brain uses two hormones—serotonin and norepinephrine—as neurotransmitters for proper brain communication and function. When these hormones are disrupted, they affect not only the brain but also the body. This can affect mood, appetite, sleep, muscles, digestion, and other functions.

Clinical depression is a multi-layered and complex mood disorder. There are various factors, including genetics, stress, circumstances, relationship, and other factors. Physiologically, these can result in altered brain chemistry, wrong belief systems, and consequently, changed mood and behaviour. [3]

Below is a list of generally agreed upon symptoms of depression.

Primary Symptom of Depression

- A sad, despairing mood that:
    - is present most days and lasts most of the day;
    - lasts for more than two weeks;
    - impairs or impedes performance at work, at school, or in social relationships (including the home).

Additional Symptoms of Depression

- Changes in appetite and weight (more than a 5 percent gain or loss of body weight)
- Sleep problems
- Loss of interest in work, hobbies, and friends
- Loss of sexual desire
- Withdrawal from family members and friends

---

[3] Lastoria, M. D. 1999. *Depression*. Edited by David G. Benner and Peter C. Hill. *Baker Encyclopedia of Psychology & Counseling*. Baker Reference Library. Grand Rapids, MI: Baker Books.

- Feelings of uselessness, hopelessness, excessive guilt, pessimism, or low self-esteem
- Agitation or lethargy
- Irritability
- Fatigue
- Trouble concentrating, remembering, and making decisions
- Susceptibility to crying easily or feeling like crying but being unable to
- Thoughts of suicide
- Self-destructive behaviour
- Loss of touch with reality, hearing voices, or having strange ideas (delusions)

One major overarching indication of depression is that nothing satisfies. You may indulge in a hobby to feel better and get no pleasure from it. You may pursue sexual activity (hopefully with your spouse) to feel better and still feel empty. Whatever coping strategies you develop, they don't provide satisfaction. You end up losing interest in most everything. Or, you jump from one pursuit to another only to find yourself still unhappy. It sounds a bit like Solomon in Ecclesiastes!

If you are experiencing a number of these symptoms and have for an extended period of time, or for more than three months, you should at minimum seek out a good therapist and perhaps seek medical attention. Drugs may be necessary, short term or long term. Sometimes drugs are not necessary as depression can be managed by implementing some healthy habits. Proper exercise, sleep, and diet are crucial to good mental health.

Just remember—there is no shame in needing help. Denial or avoidance will only exacerbate the problem.

For me personally, I did not need prescription medications, although I took St. John's Wort (an herbal remedy greatly used in Europe for the treatment of mild depression). After about a year, I weaned myself off of it —be sure to consult with a health professional before taking St. John's Wort. I made significant changes in diet and lost twenty-five pounds. I now avoid late nights and make every effort to get sufficient physical activity. I find that if I lack sleep or do not get enough exercise, I can quickly fall into a depressive state. Take care of your temple! I bought a fitness tracker to help motivate me, and it has helped. You can do something similar or partner with someone for support and accountability. It takes determination but is definitely doable if you put the right motivators, helpful routines, and a supportive network in place. The chapters that follow will outline the steps to recovery and provide information on how to prevent burnout.

CHAPTER THREE
Burnout Recovery

So What Do I Do Now?

Though the information in this chapter is helpful to all, my hope is that it will be especially beneficial to those of you who, after reading the earlier chapters and reflecting on the symptoms, believe you are close to or at the point of burnout. This discovery is often a significant and visceral moment. For some, it's like admitting to an addiction to performance or work. For others, it's a moment of fear and even panic. And still for others, it is a great sigh of relief, realizing that you now know what is really going on.

Irrespective of the experience of the moment, the question arises: What do I do now? If you believe you are at risk of burnout, the next chapter, Burnout Prevention, can provide some information and direction. If you are at a late stage or at the breaking point, some of the answers are quite simple, while others are more complex and will be covered in the chapters that follow.

It likely took months or even years to reach a point of burnout. You do not simply recover from it in a matter of weeks. It will likely take months to return to a place of restored health and productivity. Do not be discouraged by this. Quick fixes usually end in quick relapses. The question is not simply about recovery. The focus is not simply on recovery, it is also on sustainability, which is critical! You do not want to go back.

The close relationships you have will play a major role in these next steps.

DO NOT DO THIS ALONE!

Plain and simple—if you could have done it alone, you would already have figured this out, or it would never have happened in the first place. Lay down your pride. Refuse the shame. Humble yourself. And, get help. I cannot stress this enough. Your spouse and family are insufficient. Your elders and staff are insufficient. You do not go to the dentist for hernia surgery. You definitely do not ask your spouse to perform it! Unless, she's a surgeon and your marriage is healthy!

Seeing a professional Christian counsellor or therapist is a good course of action. Some denominations provide counselling or therapy as part of their benefit package. You may need your medical doctor to be involved as well if the need for medications comes into play. It is always wise to consult with your doctor. There are even Christian therapists who are available to do online counselling if you are in an isolated area.

In the pages that follow, we will look at physical, mental, spiritual, and structural areas that may need to be tackled. There is no fixed seven-step program to burnout recovery. Every individual will face various blends of factors that contributed to burnout, and that need change in order to recover.

As you examine the points below you will discover that you may need to make adjustments in your vocation. You may need time off. You may need to help your church and leadership adjust their expectations. You may need to make adjustments to job descriptions. These may seem difficult or even insurmountable, but the cost of doing nothing is far greater than the cost of making adjustments.

THE BIG MEETING

As you take next steps, perhaps one of the most frightening parts is having to talk to your governing authority and your family. The challenge is that the potential of existing unhealthy dynamics may kick in. Depending on your system of government you may face denominational involvement or simply board/elder involvement. Either way, there must be communication and the development of a plan.

In my case, I found myself in an unusually advantageous situation: my Christian therapist was also a board member of a large church, so she understood not only my condition but also church government dynamics. This was, for me, a double-blessing. She not only met with me for counselling but also met with my board to help them understand and navigate the process. Our interim pastor, Andrew, also met with her to get direction and help for the church's process of adapting and for my process of recovery. The entire procedure took one year. That may sound intimidatingly long, but that is from the start of the recovery process to my full restoration as lead pastor—with some portfolio adjustments.

If you are the pastor: Avoiding meeting with your leadership team will only make things worse. You may want to have someone from outside accompany you as a support (a friend, pastor-friend, counsellor). Prepare ahead of time what you want to say. Keep your cool, and stand your ground. Perhaps include some information on burnout that may help your team with understanding—maybe even this book! If your denomination has an official process for such situations, use it. It may be advisable to have something from a doctor or therapist on paper to help validate both your situation and the need to make changes. Your doctor may even write a prescription for a stress leave.

If you are the board: If you are recognizing burnout in your pastor, approach him with care and gentleness. Assist him in getting the help he needs. If he has come to you, do not be quick to judge or look for cause or blame. This is a particularly vulnerable moment for your pastor. It is not the time to troubleshoot the church systems—at least not at this moment. There will be a time to assess and adjust ministry dynamics during the process. PLEASE HEAR ME: If your pastor has come to you speaking of burnout, do not minimize it. Do not tell him to pray more, read more, study more, or do anything more. Start by listening. This is a critical moment, which, if handled well, can bring healing to the pastor and blessing to the church. If handled wrongly, this moment can be devastating to the pastor, his family, and the church. Respond like Jesus, not like the Pharisees.

Talking to your family is another significant step. You may experience a deep sense of failure and shame as you speak to your spouse and children about this. You may experience fear of what their reactions will be. Your family has most likely been experiencing the effects of your burnout—your behavioural and attitudinal changes. I suspect that for most, the family will express a certain level of relief that the truth is out, and you will be getting rest and help. If your marriage is under strain, you may want to get some counselling together to work through the process. My wife went to see the same therapist as I was seeing. She went separately to get advice as to how to relate and respond to me during this difficult time. I am so thankful for my wife's grace toward me!

I was quite afraid to tell my wife. The sense of failure I felt was strong, and the fear that accompanied it was equally strong. I was afraid of rejection or some type of confirmation that, Yes, you are a failure. I was so relieved to have her respond to me with acceptance and love. I had already seen my therapist before telling my wife. She advised me on how to communicate with her.

If you have children, their responses will vary according to age and personality. Use wisdom regarding what information to share and what to guard them from. I have three adult children. They all responded differently based on their personalities, their coping strategies, and their grasp of the situation. Responses ranged from avoidance to close support. They all gave me the space I needed, and they were all there when I needed them. I have great kids!

Just understand that your burnout is not their burden to carry. Give them room to work through it in their own way—within reason.

These meetings, with your leadership team, your spouse, and your children, may all be difficult but are absolutely necessary to moving forward in healing.

Why?

So how did I get here? This may be one of the many questions you currently face, along with others like:

- If God calls, doesn't he equip? Or, how could God let this happen to me?
- What about the power of the Holy Spirit in me?
- Was I out of God's will?
- Is this the devil?

I remember sitting on my deck in the first weeks of my time off. At one point, I had a significant emotional moment of prayer. God, I gave you my whole heart, my whole life! How could you let this happen to me? Is this what I get for total surrender? I believed that if I gave all and followed the call, you would protect me from such things. It was a visceral, but not at all cathartic, moment.

You will have moments where questions and doubts will arise about God's call on your life and the causes of your current situation. Just remember—in these moments you cannot fully trust your emotions or your reasonings. That's why you do not do this alone.

We live in a society that is bent on understanding cause and assigning blame. This is part of our need to be in control, or at least reconcile in our minds what we don't understand. Was it this? Was is that? There are likely several factors and not just one that lead to burnout. The important thing is to focus on resting, healing, and learning new ways of doing things to avert a recurrence in the future.

It is clear in Scripture that even Jesus was exhausted at times. When he was, he rested. You have to be pretty tired to sleep through a rough storm in a small boat!

Know that God has not abandoned you. If anything, this is a time where you may experience his mercy and grace in new ways. You will likely see God, yourself, and others in new ways that bring life to you and those around you. As far as those nagging questions go, you may or may not discover the answers to them. At this point it is more important to trust God moving forward than to have everything figured out.

Board members: Please know that your pastor is particularly vulnerable to head games at this point, and it is vitally important that you not add to them. If he vents and even says harsh things to you as elder/board members, don't be quick to judge him on it. Be patient, understanding that in the same way a person may cry out in pain when breaking a leg, he is crying out in pain from brokenness of soul.

Rest

> *So then, there remains a Sabbath rest for the people of God, for whoever has entered God's rest has also rested from his works as God did from his. (Hebrews 4:9–10, ESV)*

God has called us into a state of rest called "Sabbath". It's a place where our strength comes from God and not us. It's a place where grace flows out of a heart that is full. If you are burned out, you are not functioning in sabbath rest.

The question of rest is a big one in this context. Reaching this place in life and ministry forces a series of significant questions:

- Do I need time off? If so, how much?
- Do I need to change churches? Vocations?
- Do expectations need to change? (Mine, my family's, the ministry's?) Does the church need to change its expectations?

The first question is critical and should be addressed before the others: Do I need time off?

My first and simplest answer is yes. Ask yourself this question, If I continue as I am, will I trend upward toward health or downward toward deeper burnout and perhaps crisis? You are likely running on fumes and pure obedience to God. You likely have lost your joy. You likely feel drained most of the time. You need rest! Believe me, you do!

Rest is so important for recovery and ongoing health that I will cover it in depth in several sections of this book. The long-term goal of burnout recovery is sustainability. Of what use is it to recover only to plunge headlong back into the same situation?

I find it interesting that God's response to Elijah's low point was to provide him food and sleep, twice in 1 Kings 19.

When I began my leave of absence, my therapist told to me spend the first couple of weeks simply resting. She also told me to avoid depressive behaviour. In other words, not to sleep the days away. Rather, I was to take short walks, sit on the deck, enjoy the fresh air, read a bit, listen to music—whatever was restful to me in the moment. My capacity for handling stress was so low that I avoided even the slightest tension in any family conversation. My wife gave me space and support, what I needed, when I needed it. The kids gave me space. It was a time of just breathing. Those first few weeks I did little Bible reading or serious praying. I just rested. I rested in God's presence—not feeling it but knowing it was there. I described it this way, I don't feel close to God, but I know He is close to me. There was a definite sense of being safe with God.

On the other hand, I really struggled with being still. I felt so unproductive, so useless. Then on one of those days I felt as if God spoke to me: I am pleased with you —that you are doing nothing, because that is what you need right now. It was freeing. "For he knows our frame; he remembers that we are dust." (Psalms 103:14, ESV)

Each situation and circumstance will present opportunities and challenges that will shape your next steps as far as rest is concerned. Just remember this, you cannot shortcut this part of the process. There is no cheat for this. You may need a leave of absence. You may need an extended vacation. You may need to resign. I don't know what your next step is. Don't make it alone. It would be wise to have a counsellor work with you in this process. It may also be that your doctor will prescribe time off. If you have insurance, it will help you and the church financially during this process.

My therapist said to me, "You really don't know how heavy the load is until you put it down." So true! I didn't realize the weight I was carrying, some of it self-imposed. I had pastored the church for so long (twenty-nine years) that I was not aware of the codependency I had developed with it. I not only needed rest, I needed disengagement.

Rest is not just about time off. It is also about disengagement. It is about creating boundaries that separate you from your congregation at large. You may have a few very key relationships that feed you, which you will want to maintain. But overall, you need space, and you need to reduce your social circle to the few people whom you trust most and who are life-giving.

When it comes to the latter, it's important to know that even those close relationships may be draining at times simply because of your reduced energy level. I have always been an outgoing social type. Yet I found that in this condition, even a one-hour coffee with a friend left me exhausted. It's about maintaining a balance between healthy social interaction and healthy solitude.

You will need to work with your counsellor, church leadership, doctor, and family to determine how much time off you need. You will also likely have to return to work incrementally. It is also important that systems and boundaries are in place upon your return to guard you from falling back into burnout.

Do not be discouraged by this, but statistically it takes as much as two years to be fully restored, and that restoration is often to 80 percent of your previous 100 percent. This is not a negative thing: your previous 100 percent got you into trouble to start with. The key is energy management which will be discussed later.

I was off for two months before attending my church on Sunday mornings, not as pastor, but simply as part of the community of believers. Boundaries were set from the platform. People were asked not to initiate conversation with me, but to allow me to initiate what I was capable of. In the beginning of this phase, I left immediately following the service and was exhausted for the rest of the day.

In the fifth month, I began going into the office for up to one day per week. I chose what I could do—mostly simple, low-stress tasks. For me, that was technical work such as website maintenance and sound equipment maintenance.

At the end of the sixth month, I preached my first message in the church. By then I was going into the office two days/week. During that time I did not function as lead pastor. I was more like the employee of the interim pastor. He was very good at keeping track of my health and adjusting accordingly. If I was tired part way through the day, I went home. There was a lot of flexibility and grace. I thank God for our elders, board, and staff who were such a great leadership team.

The next two months I preached twice a month.

In the ninth month I became the primary communicator in the church and preached two to three times a month. I have never returned to preaching every Sunday. Also, I moved to three-quarter time at the office.

It was a full year later from my initial leave of absence before I was reinstated as lead pastor. However, my role has been redefined, and the interim pastor is now the associate pastor. We have learned to lean into our gifts in a complementary fashion and are both healthier for it, as is the church.

Your journey will likely be different. We are all in different circumstances. We all handle pressure differently. We all recover differently.

If you are not a pastor but part of your church's leadership team, please understand that you play a key role in restoring the soul of one who is called by God and has great value in his sight. Understand that a healthy pastor brings health to a congregation. Know that you play a key role in his recovery—or his ruin. See the big picture, and take the necessary steps and even risks to bring restoration to the pastor and to congregational health. Give him rest.

Physical

As human beings we are so intertwined physically, mentally, emotionally, and spiritually that there is no way we can stop one area from affecting the others. As such, we must examine every dimension of our being to troubleshoot our burnout and rectify what is damaging to us.

Our bodies are temples of the Holy Spirit and are meant to be taken care of and treated with value and respect. Burnout has physical repercussions on our health. Therefore, it is vital that we take proper care of ourselves physically. It will benefit not only our bodies but also our minds.

Rest

God instituted rest from the beginning of creation as a necessary part of our makeup. When we neglect it, we neglect God's design for us. When we don't get sufficient rest, we move into a process of depletion. The rate of depletion will vary for each person. The trap is when the rate of depletion is slow enough to go unnoticed. A little bit less energy here, a little less there. Then what was gradual seems like a sudden fall from maintaining to complete depletion.

We all know the simple financial math that if you spend more than you make, you run out of money. At that point, people often borrow and set themselves up for a life of bondage and debt. The problem with energy is that when you run out, you can't borrow it from someone else. There is no energy credit card!

The only way to replenish our stores of energy is through rest.

Depending on the level of burnout you are experiencing, you may have a need for a significant period of physical rest disengaged from most of life's activities. Others may simply need to schedule regular cycles of rest.

In my case, I needed an extended time of significant rest. I was depleted physically, emotionally, socially, and spiritually. I spent several weeks doing only the simplest things—going for short walks, doing a bit of reading, listening to music, and mostly sitting on my patio and staring at trees. I was instructed to avoid one particular depressive behaviour—sleeping long periods during the day. Short naps, a maximum of twenty minutes, were acceptable. My conversations varied in length and were limited to only a very select few people, my wife being the primary one. I am thankful for her patience.

As I began moving forward in energy replenishment, I went out more. I had more conversations with people. I traveled a bit on my vacation time. The whole time I had to pay close attention to energy levels—more on that later.

To this day I must still monitor my energy levels and guard my rest.

Rest Periods

The best way to maintain physical health and stamina regarding rest is to establish cycles of rest. These help maintain a discipline of rest that can assist in restoration as well as maintenance of health.

Daily Rest

The first and most important aspect of daily rest is sleep. Your body needs sleep. Your brain needs sleep. Even though sleep needs vary from person to person, many people live chronically sleep-deprived. According to the *American Sleep Association Online*, 37–40 percent of adults report short sleep duration. The results are reductions in judgment, impulse control, attention, visual association, and high function cognitive skills. We can all manage a late night. It's the accumulation of sleep deprivation that causes damage. The average adult needs seven to nine hours of sleep. Don't fool yourself into thinking you can get by with five or six hours for more than a day.

One of my personal weaknesses that contributed to burnout was staying up late when my wife went to bed early. I would watch a movie or play video games—mindless time wasters. But time flies when you're having fun! I would end up getting to bed on average between 11:00 pm and 12:30 am. Then getting up regularly at 6:30 am resulted in sleep deprivation, which had several adverse affects, such as those listed above. My wife can tell when I lack sleep before I can. She provides a good feedback system when I have too many late nights in a row. I think I can push through it, but she sees the impairment. Ongoing sleep deprivation may not seem like a big deal but it weakens the soul and makes us vulnerable to temptation, irrational thinking, and a mess of other traps.

Managing sleep is a part of managing energy. Even Jesus withdrew to rest. As I referenced earlier, when I think of the account of the storm in Matthew 8, I am stricken by the fact that Jesus was sound asleep in the middle of a storm! Was he that tired? He obviously knew he needed sleep. We are not superior to Jesus and need sleep also.

The second aspect of daily rest is incorporating a short period of disengagement into our schedules. We are all guilty of the working lunch, the working dinner, the phone call during the commute, the device on hand in the bathroom! Well, maybe not everyone on that last one. The point is, we need a time during the day where we can disengage physically and mentally from the job. We have lost the art of cave time—staring at the fire—thinking about, nothing. Take time during the day to disengage and be at peace. This is a challenge given our task-oriented society, but it is healthy.

Weekly Rest

Once a week, take a day off! It's not that you do nothing on that day—although there are the odd days I do exactly that. You are resting from the work of ministry. This belongs as much in the mental/emotional category as the physical one.

Setting a boundary for a day off may prove more challenging for some than others. It's amazing how someone who has a problem that has taken years to accumulate, decides their moment of crisis is on your day off. Most of the time it can wait. A long time ago I communicated to my congregation that my day off was not to be disturbed unless someone was dead or dying. I check call display and only answer if it's a leader calling because I know they understand the boundaries and treat those boundaries with respect.

In addition to taking a weekly day off, you would do well to take an additional day or even two in a given month. You may also plan a low-energy workday after an unusually busy week.

Annual Rest

Vacation time is a must. It's non-negotiable. Depending on the level of activity and stress in your life and ministry, you need at least three weeks of vacation time every year. I would strongly suggest that you take two weeks at one time. It often takes a minimum of three to seven days to unwind before you can actually fully relax. You don't begin to recharge until after that wind-down time. Two weeks of vacation gives you seven to eleven days of actual rest.

Find what you love to do. Find what recharges you. Find what builds your marriage and family. For some it's travel. For others, it's sitting at a campsite and reading fiction. Still, for others it's climbing a mountain or cross-country cycling. If home renovation energizes you, tackle a project. If it drains you, don't spend all of your vacation time on it. Whatever it is, do what will bring you back recharged and not exhausted. We've all had the vacation where we returned needing a vacation from our vacation to recover from a different form of fatigue. There is a time for a working vacation or a fast-paced one as well, but don't make every vacation a tiring one.

Sabbatical

Sabbaticals are an essential part of ministry health. They can consist of frequent short times off, such as three days per quarter. On the other hand, they can be long bouts away from ministry duties, such a one year every seven or two months every three years. They may be educational entailing education upgrades, research, or book writing. They can also be complete ministry disengagement. They serve the primary function of allowing you to disengage from the regular duties of ministry and are distinct from vacation time.

Physical Activity

Pastoring is generally a sedentary profession. We sit and read. We sit and study. We sit and counsel. We sit and visit. We sit at a coffee shop and talk. We sit and make phone calls. We sit in meetings. We sit and do our devotions. Sometimes it seems the most physical part of our job is standing still and talking, which, by the way, is not actually exercise—unless you're an aerobic preacher!

Our bodies need activity to be healthy. Our hearts need to work beyond basal metabolic rates to be healthy. We need physical activity! We need exercise.

Some of the health risks created by a lack of physical activity as mentioned in *Johns Hopkins Medicine Online* are as such:

- Increased risk of hypertension (high blood pressure)
- Increased feelings of anxiety and depression
- Possible increase in the risk of certain cancers
- Increased risk of disease in general

Regular physical activity helps your heart, builds your stamina, and even strengthens your concentration and mental clarity. On top of that, you burn calories, helping in the maintenance of healthy weight.

When I was on leave, I was instructed to walk every day. Fortunately, it was late spring leading in to summer, so the weather was suited to doing it (I don't like the cold). Initially, my walks were fairly slow and short (less than two km). However, over time I began to walk more briskly, and farther. My stamina increased, and I began feeling energized by the walking. I found that on the days I walked I felt more energetic and was in a better frame of mind. My thoughts were clearer. I was sharper. I could control my emotions better. Walking had much more than simply a physical effect.

You should consult with your physician when entering into new exercise practices. Ideally, a full checkup would be an important part of this process to rule out any other causes or factors that may have contributed to your burnout. Walking is the simplest and most accessible form of exercise. However, you may want to cycle or take up a sport. Just do something to get your heart rate up and your blood circulating!

Diet

Food! We have a saying among the pastors in our city: If you feed them, they will come. Much of the church's culture revolves around, or at least includes, food. This is understandable given that the Bible is full of examples of relationships built around food. Food provides a significant basis for connection between people in the church in the same way dinner with the family is a vital part of relational health.

However, the problem is not that we eat food. The problem is that we eat too much of the wrong kind. An article on ChurchLeaders.com outlines many recent studies. One study showed that evangelical Christians have the highest obesity rates of all religious groups. Another study showed that "young adults who attend church or a bible [sic] study once a week are 50 percent more likely to be obese." Pastors have a 10 percent higher obesity rate than the American national average.[4]

---

[4] Ridgaway, Toni. 2012. "Are Churches a 'Feeding Ground' for Obesity?". ChurchLeaders. Last modified June 5, 2012.
https://churchleaders.com/pastors/pastor-articles/161342-doctor-calls-churches-a-feeding-ground-for-obesity.html.

One third of American pastors are obese[5]. These statistics are alarming!

Our general attitude toward food, gluttony, and weight further complicates the role eating plays in our lives. For many of us, food has become the "drug of choice". It doesn't carry the taboo of alcohol or sexual addiction, yet it can still be an addiction. We often eat because we are bored, tired, lonely, or sad; sometimes it's for comfort, other times for celebration. Then simply, we eat because it's easy, pleasurable, and accessible.

I was experiencing what is called creeping obesity over a period of years before I came to this crisis. I gained a few pounds each year. The rate was fairly consistent with a few jumps over the Christmas holidays and summers. Steak on the BBQ! Food was not the first thing I tackled when recovering from burnout. Actually, it was one of the last. I focused mainly on exercise because along with getting my soul back to health, that's all I had strength for. Once I built up these areas, I knew I had to work on improving my diet and losing weight.

The key to changing my eating habits was the realization that food could become an idol—as it had for me. This caused me to see food and my eating habits as something directly connected to my relationship with God. It was sin, plain and simple.

---

[5] Caba, Justin. 2015. "Clergy Members Battle Obesity." Medical Daily. Last modified Jan 13, 2015. https://www.medicaldaily.com/clergy-members-battle-obesity-one-third-pastors-us-are-obese-317616.

Understand this, you don't have to be obese to have food as an idol. You don't even have to be overweight. The idolatry of food is about using food to fill the longings of your soul.

The first, and most simple approach is this: Decrease input, increase output. Burn more calories, ingest fewer calories. Adjust your portion sizes. Reduce snacking. It is amazing the difference it can make by simply walking more—taking daily walks, parking farther away from a building, using stairs instead of an elevator/escalator.

Diet vs. Diet

The word "diet" can mean two different things. There is a difference between saying, I'm on a diet, and I have changed my diet. A diet can be a time-limited activity with the goal of losing weight within that timeframe. Or, a diet can be an eating lifestyle that is intended to be permanent. If you want to get healthy and stay healthy, you cannot *go on* a diet; you must *change* your diet. This is about a new way of eating. It does not mean you will never snack again or have a second serving of turkey on Thanksgiving. It does mean you will alter what you eat, when you eat, and how much you eat, based on what is healthy for you.

Making all the changes you need at once may seem overwhelming. You do not want to set yourself up to fail. Decide how you will incrementally make the changes. Devise a plan. Stick to the plan.

Consider the change permanent. Grieve the loss. Celebrate the upcoming victories!

Healthy Approaches

Although this is not a book on nutrition it is worth mentioning that it's not only how much food you eat that matters, it's also what type of food you eat. There is plenty of information available to help you navigate a healthy diet. It may also be wise to consult with your doctor or a dietitian for advice. As you work to change your habits, consider things like calorie density (thirty potato chips have the same number of calories as twelve carrots!), fats, proteins, processed vs. unprocessed foods. Portion size and frequency of eating are also factors in weight control and overall health.

Pastors often fall prey to restaurant eating. Lunches with people and eating on the go can be your nemesis. Restaurants tend to give larger portions than what you need. Plan to take some home; just eat two thirds of the portion. This has been a challenge for me because I was taught to finish everything on my plate.

This is not the end of enjoyable eating. It is learning to enjoy more by paying attention. Savour every bite!

Medical Issues

We generally don't like to face the possibility of medical issues contributing to our condition of burnout. However, there are several conditions that can very directly contribute to, or accompany burnout.

Get a physical examination by your doctor and discuss your symptoms with him. You may be dealing with chemical imbalances, glandular issues, allergies, or other illnesses. You don't fix a car with an empty fuel tank by putting more air in the tires. In the same way, if there is something not functioning properly in your body, you can't simply fix it by getting some extra rest and exercise.

It is unfortunate that in our society, people often experience shame or stigma around depression symptoms. There tends to be a taboo around medications used to treat depression or other disorders. However, we would not shame someone in need of insulin or thyroid medications. Therefore, there is no shame in needing medication to adjust for chemical imbalances. Our brain is still a physical part of us, even if it affects the cognitive and emotional parts of our lives.

Addictions

Addictions often accompany burnout. They begin as coping strategies, avoidance behaviour, and self-medicating solutions to stress. When thinking of addictions, we often immediately think of the more obvious vices such as drugs, alcohol, and sex. Addictions can take many forms. Addictions can exists in physical, emotional, and spiritual dimensions. Many addictions come as the result of the increasing desire for dopamine releases in the brain.

Consequently, addictions can range from seemingly benign things such as hobbies, video games, social media, and workaholism, to more escalated problems such as drugs, alcohol, and risky behaviours that are compulsive and uncontrollable. See MentalHelp.net/

Addiction/What-Is-It for a helpful definition of addiction.

For me, my addictions became Netflix and food, specifically snacks. I was binge watching TV programs for hours a day and snacking virtually every evening. They were forms of escape and comfort followed by guilt and mental sluggishness, which led to escape and comfort, and so on.

Don't be fooled into thinking the more benign forms of addiction are somehow less harmful. They may not take you out of the ministry as quickly, but they eventually will render you ineffective in life and ministry.

Food addiction will reduce your energy levels and overall health. Digital addictions, such as gaming, video, and social media will rob you of time and leave you feeling guilty. You will be mentally distracted and less spiritually sensitive. Addictions dull your heart. Workaholism will hurt you and your family. Your relationships will suffer as will your sleep. You will still be unsatisfied no matter how much work you get done. More importantly, you will lose the ability to rest in God and to still your soul.

As you can see, each addiction has its own way of robbing your spirit, soul, and body. If you have an addiction, get help. If you think you have none, ask someone you trust to tell you the truth in case you are in denial.

Breaking addiction requires work, support, and the grace of God, but it is vital to your wholeness.

Mental/Emotional

We have already looked at the physical effects of burnout. In addition to these, we are profoundly affected mentally and emotionally when we approach or experience burnout. We lose mental acuity. We experience shame and guilt. We experience uncontrollable emotions or no emotion at all. We have greater difficulty problem-solving. We cannot stay focused or become obsessively focused.

There is no fixed pattern or set of symptoms. As individuals we experience burnout uniquely.

It is vital to take steps to restore your soul to health. Your mind and emotions are likely worn and frayed. God's design for all of us is to live out of His peace—and burnout takes us far from it.

Mental

It is difficult to break your whole being down into separate components since they interact and affect one another. The physical can affect the mental. The emotional can affect the spiritual. We are not nearly as compartmental as we'd like to be.

Our thoughts are major contributors to our condition and to our behaviour. Recovering from burnout involves a significant amount of adjustment to our thinking. By the time we burn out, we are already thinking in ways that are toxic and harmful. Our thoughts toward ministry, others, and ourselves become distorted and out of perspective. This is often the place where lies lodge themselves into our thinking, and we spend far too much time dwelling on them.

When you are burned out, your mind needs a combination of rest, stimulation, and focus.

Rest

Stress disengagement is vital to resting the mind. As mentioned earlier in this chapter, it may be necessary to for you to disengage from whatever brings significant stress into your life. This may constitute a leave of absence or a reduction of responsibilities. At home, it may involve increasing your down time. It may involve inviting someone else into your world to help manage your life's affairs—finances, work around the house, whatever triggers unnecessary stress.

Recreation is another important source of mental rest. Hobbies and healthy distractions like fishing, cycling, photography, and carpentry are good to take your mind off the things that are overwhelmingly weighty. For me, cooking was the hobby I chose to rest my mind from other things. I also spent much time simply sitting outside and watching nature.

Stimulation

Stimulation would seem to be the opposite of rest. However, it is not generally healthy to allow the mind endless idle time. Take time to rest your mind, then also take time to stimulate it. The temptation might be to read work-related books or engage in ministry-related study. However, this will too easily lead you back to the ministry mindset—from which you are resting.

Cooking was my choice of hobby, not simply because I like to cook, or to eat for that matter, but because of my interest in the chemistry of food and cooking. I took a course on cooking science. I read about the composition of foods and the chemical reactions that take place when they are mixed and heated. It was all intriguing to me! It's interesting how doing this provided both rest and stimulation for my mind. It was relaxing and invigorating at the same time! This hobby may sound like something you'd avoid like the plague. Nonetheless, find something that will stimulate your mind. Learn something new—something that interests you. It's good to keep the mind engaged.

Focus

Focus is likely the most important of these three areas being pointed out. Focus is about what you pay attention to. What you pay attention to is what you reinforce. It is about what occupies your mind the most. Meditation as described in the Bible, is a form of focus and is strongly encouraged. Scripture often uses the language of meditation to describe it. Perhaps one of the most important passages is Philippians 4:8.

> *Finally, brothers and sisters, whatever is true, whatever is noble, whatever is right, whatever is pure, whatever is lovely, whatever is admirable—if anything is excellent or praiseworthy—think about such things.*

"Whatever is true." Burnout is filled with lies—about you, about others, about ministry, about God. Meditation is a mental discipline to stay focused on truth when the lies shout so loudly in the mind. I needed the help of a counsellor to grasp truth again. Along with that, I needed to will myself into focusing on those truths. "Jesus loves me! This I know, for the Bible tells me so." We learned it in Sunday school as kids. Yet it is such a profound truth. I spent considerable time just reminding myself of that truth. It became my "sword of the Spirit" against all the thoughts of failure and inadequacy. It was my weapon against performance pressure. It was my rock of truth against the fears of an uncertain future.

One of the dangers of an unfocused mind is imagination. You can greatly entertain yourself with imaginations of you and others dying, your family falling apart, your ministry life ending. You can get stuck in imagining yourself in adulterous situations or in a variety of sins. You can swim in a sea of negative outcome-based fantasies. Instead, feed your imagination with positive or at least neutral ideations.

If you based your identity on anything other than being God's dearly loved child, you must reject it as a lie. Accept the truth that God loves you as much in this moment of burnout as He did when you were at full performance. He loves you as much now as He did when you said you'd serve Him with all your heart. He loves you as much now as at your peak moments of fruitfulness. Think on these things.

Emotional

Emotions can be very tricky to navigate. We in the world of Christian faith are often taught to hold our emotions suspect. We are definitely told that they are tertiary to faith and truth. Yet emotions can hold such sway in our lives. It is reasonable for me to expect emotions toward my wife. My love is more than simply cognitive. I expect to experience emotions when one of my children does something of which I am proud. Emotions can be your friend and ally. They can also be your greatest enemies.

I will experience emotions when I find out I've disappointed someone I care about. I will experience emotions when something I try doesn't turn out as expected. We are not immune to emotions, be it positive or negative.

Emotions are like a dashboard in a car. They can warn you of something dangerous such as an overheated engine. They can simply inform you of something, as a high-beam indicator does. They can even tell you something approving. I have an indicator on my dashboard that says Ready to Drive. Anger over an injustice is not a wrong emotion. Anger over losing at a game is. It's the same emotion driven by a different cause. The emotion is just the indicator of how we are interpreting the situation.

When we believe lies, when we lose hope, when we hold offences, we experience emotions that, if believed and embraced, are harmful to us. It is our response to our emotions that ultimately determine their power in our lives.

About two weeks into my leave, I was sitting outside on the deck just resting. All at once this thought, along with its matching emotion, came: God, I gave my whole life to do your will. I sacrificed. I persevered. I have served you. I have loved you with all my heart. How could you let this happen to me? Is this my reward for serving you wholeheartedly?

Who would dare speak to God that way? Actually, people like Moses, David, Elijah. God seems okay with us pouring out our hearts to Him, even when the thoughts are not based in truth. However, had I anchored myself in those emotions and thoughts, I would likely have become bitter toward God. The thoughts and feelings didn't leave right away. I did wrestle with them for a day or two. Yet in the midst of my struggle, I reminded myself that God loved me and was with me through it all. Choosing truth while processing pain brought the anchor I needed to get through it. The following thought was critical in finding freedom from this moment.

Forgiveness

This may sound strange, but I had to forgive God. Of course, God needs no forgiveness for he cannot sin against anyone. God didn't owe me an explanation or anything else for that matter. What I mean is this: I had to stop blaming God. I'm using the word forgiveness in the sense of letting go. Whether it be God, church leadership, congregants, your spouse, or anyone else, you cannot afford to hold on to blame. It is an emotional cesspool filled with poison for the soul.

Please forgive. Forgive yourself. Forgive others. Forgive God. Don't spend all your emotional energy on cause and blame. Even if you were genuinely wronged, unforgiveness will not help you in any way.

Thankfulness

Usually the last thing you feel when burned out is thankful. Right. Thank you Lord for my burnout. I get it.

Thankfulness is more of an attitude than an emotion. It also begins with a choice, not a mood. We choose to be thankful. Oftentimes gratitude, as an emotion, follows the choice.

I began moving toward thankfulness with the anchor thought mentioned earlier—Jesus loves me. I began being thankful that God still loved me, despite my feelings of failure and my lack of performance. I expressed my thankfulness for being his child, for having eternal life, for receiving my salvation. The concept is simple, but it's the starting point for all other areas of life. After all, isn't our salvation the most important thing in life?

It's amazing how much expressing my thankfulness for God's love in words, became a healing salve for my emotions. I felt gratitude, and even more importantly, hope rose from within. I began to actually believe I was going to be okay. I was going to survive. This was not just hope. It was a door for peace to enter my heart.

This didn't happen all at once. And, it was not the order of the day every day. Thankfulness was the slow climb up the hill toward healthy emotions.

Final Thought

Both your thoughts and emotions are the battlegrounds of guilt and shame. Guilt and shame are the weapons of the enemy to keep you from getting back up and winning this war. To finish this section read this passage from Zechariah 3:1–5.

> *Then he showed me Joshua the high priest standing before the angel of the Lord, and Satan standing at his right side to accuse him. The Lord said to Satan, "The Lord rebuke you, Satan! The Lord, who has chosen Jerusalem, rebuke you! Is not this man a burning stick snatched from the fire?" Now Joshua was dressed in filthy clothes as he stood before the angel. The angel said to those who were standing before him, "Take off his filthy clothes." Then he said to Joshua, "See, I have taken away your sin, and I will put fine garments on you." Then I said, "Put a clean turban on his head." So they put a clean turban on his head and clothed him, while the angel of the Lord stood by.*

Shame is not your due when you open up your heart to God. His desire is your restoration and health!

Spiritual

If you are on the edge or at the point of burnout, you are spiritually vulnerable. Temptation, despair, even loss of faith are dangers at this point. It is not unusual to begin to question your call, or even your entire belief system. It is vitally important to have spiritual anchor points in your life during this pivotal time.

Anchor Points

> *God did this so that, by two unchangeable things in which it is impossible for God to lie, we who have fled to take hold of the hope set before us may be greatly encouraged. We have this hope as an anchor for the soul, firm and secure. It enters the inner sanctuary behind the curtain, where our forerunner, Jesus, has entered on our behalf. He has become a high priest forever, in the order of Melchizedek. (Hebrews 6:18–20)*

First, and most importantly, our anchor is in Jesus Christ. This truth is vital to successful recovery. Your relationship with God is not contingent on your present condition. It is based in on your faith and trust in God.

This is the time where the verses you learned in Sunday school and throughout life are vital to your stability. Ephesians 2:8–9, John 3:16, 1 John 1:9, and the like are so important to anchoring yourself to the truth of God's word.

Times of burnout are times of questioning and doubt. God's word is the constant in your life. Remind yourself and make this about truth, not about feelings.

The Old Testament has several accounts where people used objects as reminders, or memorials, of something God said or did. Several psalms speak of remembering the things God has done. This is a time to go back to some of the key times in your life when you had significant moments with God—times when you saw God do something great in your life or circle, times when you sensed God speaking to you clearly, times when you were assured of your call to ministry, times of deep devotion and surrender, times of obedience and resulting fruitfulness. These all provide the memorials of God's word and work in your life. Recount them. Reflect on them. Relive them. Rejoice in them.

Biblical Reset

I remember seeing a Kellogg's Corn Flakes commercial that basically used the slogan, "Kellogg's Corn Flakes—Taste them again for the first time." It was a great marketing strategy to invite people to revisit their old breakfast cereal as if it was a fresh new product. I found myself craving corn flakes!

I would suggest this: The Bible—Read it again for the first time. One of the detriments of burnout in ministry, especially for those who's role is communicating the Word of God regularly, is that the Bible becomes so much of a tool, that it is no longer the well we drink from.

As much as I exhorted others not to, I found myself reading the Bible primarily for sermon content and little for personal devotion and enrichment. Even when doing my own devotional reading, anything that really stuck out or revealed something new was quickly followed by the thoughts: I wonder how this would preach? I wonder if I should do a series on this? I wonder if so and so needs to hear this? and so on. It's not that there was no appreciation for what I was seeing, it's just that I always funnelled it into ministry. This is not feeding on God's word for ourselves!

There is nothing wrong with a Sunday message coming out of devotional reading. The danger is when most or all of our devotional reading becomes about ministry content.

When I first took my leave of absence, I had no desire to read the Bible. I had no energy to read the Bible. My counsellor affirmed that I probably have more of the Bible stored up in my heart than many people have in their entire lifetime. A bit of time without Bible reading was not going to cause everything I already knew and believed to drain out.

After a few weeks of rest, I began to read a bit at a time. However, I began to read the Bible differently. I purposed in my heart to read the Bible as if it was new to me. I decided to read each passage as a kid who didn't have all the personal history of study and assumptions. It became fresh, new, and life-giving in a way I hadn't experienced in years! We can become so familiar with and knowledgeable of Scripture that we can no longer see past the existing framework of our internalized theology. Not that our theology would change as a result of reading with new eyes, but that we become blinded by what we already know.

Become a child again and rediscover the awe and mystery of the Bible. See every story, every miracle, every statement, as something fresh and new to be discovered all over again. If need be, read a different translation for a fresh experience.

I have found that since doing this, not only has my devotional life been fresher, my teaching ministry has become more vibrant. I love the Word of God once again!

Prayer Life

Prayer can be a strange thing for people in ministry. It can be a joy. It can be work. It can be tedious. It can be energizing. Nevertheless, it IS vital!

It is most likely that your prayer life has been deeply affected during this time. You may have found yourself praying more, praying less, not praying, pleading with God, rebuking the devil, and whatever else. You probably have felt quite ineffective—at least regarding prayer for yourself.

It's easy for people to say, "You should have prayed more or harder." Hearing this just adds to the existing feelings of failure and discouragement. It's not that simple. Yes, prayer is vital, but restless anxious prayer is exhausting. Rest is as important as prayer. Even Jesus took time to rest and not pray. One is not a replacement for the other. Both are necessary.

So what now? How do you restore your prayer life? Or build a new one?

- Complete honesty without restraint: Over sixty psalms contain laments. Many people in the Bible complained honestly to God and he responded in love and with care. He intervened, provided answers, gave perspective, and even gave promises.

- Faith: Hebrews 11:6 says, "And without faith it is impossible to please God, because anyone who comes to him must believe that he exists and that he rewards those who earnestly seek him." Prayer is about faith. Faith is demonstrated in approaching God and seeing Him as your source. He knows your state. He can take your laments. Be honest with Him about your thoughts and feelings. Also remember to frame it all in truth—what does God's word say about you as a child of God.
- Simplicity: Prayer does not need to be complicated. Start simple. Be conversational. Find what helps you best to pray: taking a walk, listening to music, going for a drive, whatever catalyses your prayer.
- Silence (listening prayer): I have found the most challenging part of prayer is stillness and silence. Yet these are times where I often experience real peace, and my heart and mind become clear. Take some time to just listen. Even if God doesn't speak, he is there.

You will find that, over time, prayer will become a living well for your soul. It will be the place where you truly experience God's presence in such a way that you will actually start to crave it.

Structural

It Takes A Village

In recovery, it is often necessary to change some of the structures around your life and ministry. The topics covered earlier in this chapter, as well as those in the next chapter, can serve as guideposts to setting new boundaries and establishing new structures. Making changes requires determination and discipline. It is quite easy to revert to old ways of doing things, and the temptation to do so can be strong.

Changes in ministry structure also require the willingness and cooperation of all involved, from leadership to congregants. It is important to invite the congregation into the process of change. After all, a culture change will likely be needed to ensure ongoing health for both the pastor and the church. A certain level of transparency is needed in this process. The leadership needs to be clear and firm about changing boundaries. This is a cooperative effort to bring ongoing strength to the whole church.

For our church, the initial part of the process began with me creating a short six-minute video for the congregation. I did this at home and explained my need to replenish. I said, "Instead of a container overflowing I have become a pipe God flows through. There is nothing left in my own life." Note that after recording this video, I slept three hours! The head of the board read a prepared statement at the Sunday morning service followed by a presentation of the video. Then some basic ground rules were given to the congregation regarding making contact with me (as in zero contact allowed—no texts, no emails, no phone calls, no visits). The leadership was clear, positive, and reassuring to the congregation.

The leadership structure and recovery process were explained. The church's needs were made known. People stepped up and contributed! There was a gained cohesiveness and sense of working together that grew in the process. Yes, some withdrew, and a few even left. However, the net gains in producing a healthy church environment far outweighed the losses. The net increase in health was well worth the small losses.

As the process continued and I began simply attending, clear boundaries were set again; I was not functioning as part of the pastoral staff but only as a part of the community. Social space was granted to me so I could regain my energy and start connecting with people.

We made every effort to keep people informed in such a way that didn't violate my need for privacy but assured them of progress.

This is where congregational love truly gets tested. Church consumers don't fare well during these times, but a spiritual family is strengthened.

Time

During my recovery, I gradually re-engaged in work/ministry life. I didn't go from being completely off to being full-time. I began with a gradual process. Once again, the board was helpful and supportive. As my stamina and resilience increased, I moved from working two to four hours per week into the full-time role of lead pastor. This process took several months. I was completely off for two months. I then began attending the church and going into the office one to two hours per week. I preached my first message six months after taking leave. It was a full year before I was restored to the full role of lead pastor.

This process will be different for each individual. Some are able to get back to full function in much less time. The important thing is not to rush. A second burnout is typically far more severe than the first, and every effort should be made to avoid a second occurrence.

If, as a long-distance runner, you tore a ligament, you would have to build yourself back up gradually. This is the same for the soul in the case of burnout.

Portfolio

Your portfolio is your job description. I recently met a pastor who was expected to be on call seven days a week, twenty-four hours a day. He burned out twice because he was forced back too early in the recovery process. He no longer pastors but is now an addictions counsellor. He told me he would never return to pastoring—both for his sake and for his family's.

In the typical North American church of today, we have taken a spiritual gift (pastor-teacher) and turned it into a title. Many times this results in the pastor being laden with many responsibilities that are completely outside his gifting or skill set. Pastors are expected to know carpentry, family law, charity law, accounting principles, counselling, car repair, website design, and more—all on top of preaching, teaching, visiting, and praying for people. If the church was a business, the staff would all be telling the boss that he's trying to do too much, needs to delegate, and should hire specialists in their respective fields to take over much of his workload.

Churches often have tight budgets and so can't always afford to pay the specialists. However, it's wrong to just assume the pastor will learn or somehow magically know how to do so many things.

As I was in the recovery process, my associate, Andrew, and I met regularly simply to discuss what I would no longer be doing as the lead pastor. We talked about what was mine, what was his, and what was shared. We set boundaries to protect me from falling into the traps of being directly "responsible" for every aspect of the church. As we redefined our roles, some of my responsibilities changed. Whereas I used to counsel everyone in the church, I now only counsel selectively: church staff and leadership, those with whom I already had history, and those I feel the need to counsel. I do very little administration, and only where my strengths lie. I used to preach 95 percent of the time. I now preach 80 percent of the time and share that role with my associate. I used to do all the weddings along with the premarital counselling and all the funerals. Again, these are now shared.

I realize not everyone reading this has a second pastor on staff. Yet, that doesn't justify the expectation that the pastor should do everything on his own. This makes it vital for the board and/or elders to work together with the pastor to develop strategies for empowering volunteers or to make the budget sacrifice to hire some help. Still, if none of these options are even possible, then the congregation needs to change its expectation of the pastor, who is a limited human being. You want your pastor to be the best at pastoring!

The health of the pastor and the church is key, so do what is necessary to help the pastor spend the bulk of his time where he is gifted and where his strengths are. This will give him joy in the ministry, which will enable him to do some of the other things as well.

Space

When you are restructuring your work life, don't overlook the importance of physical environment. Without argument, our environment affects us. Weather, temperature, noise level, and familiar/unfamiliar spaces affect mood, among other things. What is the pastor's working environment?

Before I went on leave, I had a reasonably sized office: a desk, a chair, a rocker/recliner, chairs for others, and bookshelves. It was your typical work space. However, this office had become the place where my unhealthy coping mechanisms were practiced. Much of my binge watching took place in my office. Many of the head games I faced happened in my office. As I was returning to work, I realized this office had become a place of darkness and bad memories.

Andrew had occupied my office in the interim. When I returned, he asked if I wanted my office back, quite willing to relinquish the space. I refused. I believed the office space would be better used by him since he had more meetings with volunteers and staff. However, the primary driver in my decision was that I didn't want to regularly walk into a reminder of my dark days. I am not frightened of the office or unable to cope with it. I am not incapable of using the office. I just don't need to spend my mental and emotional energy reflecting on a painful part of my life. It's not so much avoidance—well, actually it is. I choose to avoid that office. I don't need the head games.

Instead, we have arranged for me to work where I can be most productive. I am generally in the office one day a week for meetings and administrative work. I am sometimes in the office for counselling. Aside from those three tasks, I spend most of my work hours at a place of my choosing—the place where I get the most done. I have about four different locations in the city where I go to work. I tried working from home and still do from time to time, but I find that being home too easily entangles my thoughts with household responsibilities.

A laptop, wifi, headphones, and there I have a portable office.

Again, you may not have the staff to make this happen. Nevertheless, I would suggest you look for ways to make your environment peaceful, healthy, and even uninterruptible when needed. Choose or create a healthy, productive work environment.

CHAPTER FOUR
Burnout Prevention

Energy Management

We live in a society that is highly time conscious. The level of busyness we experience requires us to manage our time well. There are many time-management courses, methods, and tools. However, what is more important to consider than time is our energy. As much as time is limited, so are our own physical, emotional, and spiritual energies. We have different capacities for energy. Regardless of how much time we may have available, we must govern our time and tasks within the boundaries of our energy.

Our problem is not time management. It is energy management. Preventing burnout then, is about sustainability of energy levels.

Stamina Vs Resilience

It's good to know the difference between stamina and resilience. Both are important and affect each other, but they are managed differently. Stamina is the ability to keep going *before* you have to stop. If you were running, stamina would be the time you could keep running without having to stop and rest. On the other hand, resilience is based on the amount of rest or recovery time you need before you can go again. If you were running, resilience would be the amount of time you needed to restore the energy necessary for you to run that length again.

Every one of us has a measure of stamina and a measure of resilience. How long can I keep going at my current level of output and stress before I have to stop to rest? This is about stamina. We have daily stamina and general stamina. I may be able to go for a certain amount of time working in ministry in a day before needing rest. However, an accumulation of daily work and stress may require me to have more than one night's rest. This is what vacations are for. They are your down time to rest and recover from accumulated work output and stress.

You will find that when you reach burnout your stamina is very low. A small amount of work becomes exhausting. Where you once could have multiple conversations with people after a church service, you can now only have a few, and you are DONE! Where you could counsel people for half or a full day, you can now barely handle one session, and you are ready to sleep the rest of the day. Where you could preach your heart out and still be ready to have people over and then preach again later that same day, you finish the service and want more than a nap—you want a small coma!

When we extend ourselves beyond our stamina, tolerance and patience are greatly reduced. You'll find you won't want to be around people who drain you. Sometimes you don't want to be around anyone—even those closest to you.

Resilience is about how long a nap you need, how long you need away from people, how long you need down time before you are ready to re-engage in ministry activities. Once again, in a burnout situation resilience is often greatly reduced. A small amount of work requires a great amount of rest(oration).

It is vitally important to understand and recognize the difference between these two concepts and how they apply to the spiritual, emotional, social, and physical areas of energy. You need to know when to stop, and you need to know how long to rest. One is not a substitute for the other.

I personally found that during recovery I needed to work for short time periods followed by longer than usual periods of rest. My stamina was low as was my resilience. As I began to improve, it was my resilience that increased first. I still could only work for short periods, but my rest and recovery time became shorter. Then, the restoration of my stamina began to increase as well.

Depending on your age, you may discover that your stamina never returns to 100 percent and that you need more frequent periods of rest. This is especially true when you enter your fifties. It's likely that 80 percent is your new 100 percent. It is vital that you adjust your expectations lest you set yourself up to burnout again, resulting in even greater damage to you and your personal world.

Multiple Gauges

If you've ever looked at a race car, you may likely have noticed multiple gauges on the dashboard. Each of those gauges show a different aspect of the engine's function. Temperature, oil pressure, oil temperature, and transmission fluid temperature are all examples of gauges that provide feedback for the healthy operation of that vehicle. If any of those levels reach critical levels, the engine is in danger of failure, and damage may occur. It doesn't matter what the engine's temperature is if you have no oil pressure. You will still damage or destroy that engine! It is vital that all the levels are within the normal parameters for optimum performance.

This is also true for us. As was mentioned earlier, there are different kinds of energy: spiritual, emotional, social, and physical. Like the race car, each of these areas shows a different aspect of our overall energy function. If any of these is too low, our mental acuity is diminished, and we cannot function optimally. We may also have a larger tank for one kind of energy. Our tendency is to lean into that area when we've depleted others. We can do this for a time but not for the long term.

Spiritual Gauge

Spiritual energy is the measure of the condition of your relationship with God. So ask yourself: Is my heart full? How am I at resisting temptation? How well equipped am I to pray for and minister to other people? Have I spent time with God in prayer and devotions? These are the spiritual gauges. In general, we have an instinctive sense of our spiritual energy. Sometimes we can also fool ourselves into thinking we have more than we actually do; watch for that. This is your lifeline; you cannot afford to neglect it.

Emotional Gauge

Emotional energy is reflected in your capacity to handle your and others' emotions. So ask yourself: Am I easily overwhelmed? Does my mood shift easily? Am I easily discouraged? If you answer yes to these questions, you likely have low emotional energy. You can also measure emotional energy by how drained you feel when dealing with others at an emotional level. Some people drain more slowly emotionally, some more quickly. How quickly are you drained when counselling someone?

Social Gauge

Social energy is what you use in social situations. For the introvert, social energy will drain far more quickly than for the extrovert. So ask yourself: How many conversations can I have until I just want to be alone?

How much people noise can I handle? Being in groups requires social energy. Even one-on-one conversations require social energy. If you are a pastor, this area is one that may have a particularly high demand with church services, counselling, meetings, and social gatherings. Pay attention.

Physical Gauge

Physical energy is often the easiest to measure because physical fatigue is self-evident. The more physically healthy you are, the greater your stamina and resilience. Much of this is covered in the previous chapter so I will not repeat it, but do ask yourself the relevant questions! Remember the importance of proper physical rest. It will ultimately affect all areas of your life.

These areas are intertwined. When your physical energy is low, you are susceptible to irritability and impatience (emotional and mental). If you are sad or discouraged, you are susceptible to temptation (spiritual, physical, mental). These areas of our being are inseparable and, as such, must all be taken into consideration when it comes to energy management.

Each area has its own stamina and resilience levels. You may have high physical stamina but low social stamina. Some of this is tied to your own makeup and personality.

People who live in rural areas understand the importance of not letting a gas tank fall below the half-way point because of the distance to the gas station and the potential need for long distance travel on a day the gas station is closed. Living in the city as I do, I regularly let my gas tank get to the red line because I live one minute from the gas station. It's not a good habit, but I still do it. We can't afford to do that with energy levels.

Here is a general rule: *Do not let any energy level drop below 25 percent.* If you do, it will affect your mental acuity as well as other areas of energy. This requires that you learn to pay attention and listen to your own spirit, soul, and body. It is vital that you be attentive to each of these areas so you can gauge what is left in your energy tank.

Policies and Demands

Now we come to the actual job or work environment and its relation to burnout. Policies, expectations (expressed and undisclosed), and culture (church or ministry) can all contribute to chronic stress. It is all too easy for churches to overlook the fact that the pastor also needs to maintain his own spiritual, emotional, and physical health. Sick people don't do well at caring for others. Therefore, policies should be in place to protect the ministry leader from burnout.

There are traps that exist for both the board—or whatever leadership structure you have—and the leader. The pastor may expect too much of himself. The board may expect too much of the pastor. The congregants may expect too much of the pastor. My therapist said this: "In your church you have 200 bosses, and each has their own job description for you." Wow! That was a wake up call. Consequently, clear boundaries need to be put in place to ensure healthy leaders and healthy congregants.

Below are a few questions to consider. The church leadership will have to discern what is best since every situation is different. When considering them, keep in mind that the goal is wholeness for the leader AND for the congregants.

- What church policies, job descriptions, and cultural demands need to be adjusted to nurture healthy ministry within the church?
- What expectations are there of the pastor on his day off and after hours?
- What expectations are there of the pastor regarding friends within and outside the church?
- What expectations should there be of the pastor's spouse and children?
- What is the balance of administrative work versus spiritual work for the pastor? How does that fit his own gift mix?
- What areas of ministry can and should the pastor delegate to other staff or volunteers so he can fulfil his primary role?
- What programs take more energy than the fruit they produce? What should be stopped?
- Does the church provide for occasional days away and sabbaticals beyond vacations for the pastor's personal rest and renewal?

Here are some of the key elements the leadership and I have come up with in support of my wellbeing:

- My board encourages me to take a few days every quarter to get away, rest, and pray.
- I have call/name display on my phone so I can screen calls, especially on my day off.
- We have set a clear boundary regarding days off: If you want my attention, you need to be dead or close to it. However, I do answer calls from staff and elders.
- I am free to have friends in the church without it being considered favouritism. These are the people I would vacation with or spend time with on my day off.
- Administrative areas where I am particularly weak are now given to others to carry out so my best energy can be spent on my primary call and gifts.
- I do not attend midweek prayer service except when I want to. This area has been given to trusted people to lead.
- I only counsel people in leadership or others I choose to. The rest of the counselling is given to my associate or referred to professionals.

These are just a few examples of boundaries that have been set, some before burnout, some after. They have allowed me to be healthier and more productive, resulting in stronger ministry and a healthier church overall.

If you are a pastor, you don't have to do it all! You are not the head of the church—Jesus is. Let the parts of the body use their gifts to work with you.

If you are a board member or part of the leadership team, don't ask your pastor to be more than what God made him to be. Realize that he needs space and rest as much as anyone else, sometimes more because of his position on the spiritual front lines of ministry.

Honour each other. Work together. Set healthy boundaries.

Relationship Management

There are three types of relationships:

- Relationships that feed
- Relationships that drain
- Relationships that are reciprocal (give/take, balanced)

Think of yourself as having a relationship bank in your soul. As long as you make larger deposits than withdrawals, you will have a positive balance. If you make greater withdrawals than deposits, you will end up with a deficit, a negative balance. When that happens, there is a cumulative cost—call it interest— which sooner or later, you will have to pay.

In our lives we have people who will deposit into, withdraw from, or balance our relationship banks. We become unhealthy when there are more withdrawals being made than deposits over a period of time. This is not based on the number of people you interact with, but the net effect of those interactions. I can interact with five people that drain me and two that feed me, yet still come out with a positive balance.

When I first burned out I was asked by my counsellor to make a list of relationships in my life and to categorize them as feeding, draining, or neutral/balancing. What I discovered was that I had a far greater number of draining relationships than feeding ones. No, I did not count my whole congregation! These were the highly interactive relationships in my life—the ones I engaged in regularly.

Overall, however, only a few key draining relationships had a the greatest effect on my net balance. A small handful of people drained more out of me than the feeding relationships could replenish. *In burnout prevention, it is wise to recognize who feeds and who drains you and to set the necessary boundaries to keep a positive balance over time.*

The first step in my recovery was to minimize my contact with draining relationships and lean into the feeding relationships. This is a simplified statement. There was a process. At first, I had no contact with draining relationships and even minimal contact with feeding relationships because my social energy was so low. This is a temporary process in burnout recovery.

It is the nature of ministry to have relationships with people that drain. It cannot be avoided. Just make sure you also have relationships that feed you. Have a mentor, a life coach, a colleague (perhaps with the gift of encouragement), a friend, a confidant. Also, remember that no human relationship can take the place of your relationship with God. Only God can fill your soul in ways people cannot.

CHAPTER FIVE
New Beginnings

Hope

It has been approximately five years since I stepped down from my position for a leave of absence; four years since my full return as lead pastor. I am in a good place today. Yet the journey was not without some hills and valleys. I would say it took close to two years before I felt I had reached my new normal for energy (80 percent is my new 100 percent). On the other hand, I have sometimes fallen into the trap of feeling so re-energized that I overextended and suffered for it. What a temptation to overreach when you feel so good!

I am still learning to pay attention. I am still catching myself neglecting some of the principles I have learned. As a result of some surgery, I gained back one-third of the weight I had lost and am still contending for that weight. These are likely challenges that will continue for some years to come. I can't rely on "personal autopilot"; it's a trap. I have to pay attention. This is about learning a new way of thinking. I don't live with a defeatist mentality, yet I have sometimes been afraid others would see me as damaged goods and not hold me in the same regard as they used to. However, I cannot control other people's perceptions of me. I am confident that God can still use me and that I have a bright future. This requires walking balanced between awareness of my own frailty and confidence in God's strength. Wisdom becomes the word of the day—every day.

I am stronger in my identity today than I was before I burned out. I understand how important it is for me to define myself by what God's word speaks rather than what people speak. This is not to say I ignore others' input into my life. It is simply that my value is no longer derived from their approval, or lack thereof. I find that I am more humble, yet confident. I realize every day that I must rely on, and trust God for His wisdom, direction, and strength for both ministry and life in general. My confidence comes from knowing he is with me and will help me. I am more productive than I have been in years, and I am clearer in focus. My thinking is clearer, albeit sometimes a bit slower. Fatigue quickly brings in fog. Conversely, when I am well rested I can perform well. My heart is filled with gratitude for all that God has done, and I have great hope for the future.

Here is the good news: ***It is not hopeless for you!***

No matter how things may look, no matter how you may feel, no matter how hopeless and dark things may seem around you, there is hope! Choose to believe that God has not forsaken you. It's the truth. Choose to believe that you will get through this.

There is more good news: If you are at the place of burnout, there is fruit on the other side well worth the effort. Initially, you may feel that it is painful—that it demands some form of sacrifice when you are already feeling drained. You may even feel overwhelmed. Yet, in the same way that we discipline our bodies to follow the painful physiotherapy routine to recover from a physical injury, we must push ourselves to take the necessary steps so we can fully recover. I cannot say it enough; it is worth it.

Identity

Since vocational ministry involves a sense of identity and not just function, there is a natural tendency for pastors and people in ministry to derive their identity and value from that ministry. It is very difficult to separate your identity from your ministry function. Every believer, vocational ministers included, must find his identity in Christ as a child of God, not in performance and activity. Our worth is because of his love, not from our efforts and deeds. The work we do flows out of our identity in Christ. (Ephesians 2:10)

In discovering my codependency on the church, I also discovered how tied up my identity was in pastoring that church. Codependency is strongly tied to identity. "Among the core characteristics of codependency is an excessive reliance on other people for approval and a sense of identity."[6] When our identity is derived from others, we fall into a need to please or to keep people's opinions of us to be what we perceive we need. Long term pastoring allowed me to define the culture of the church. What I didn't realize was that the church was also defining me. My identity became tied up in the church. Who is Marc Brule without ministry? This was a very difficult question for me to face and work through. What does it really mean to simply be a child of God? This is what I had to relearn.

There is such a freedom that comes from understanding your identity separately from your function! Walking through this process restores the fundamental truth of why Jesus calls us to be like children to inherit the Kingdom—we simply are his. Jesus invites you to know him and rediscover who you really are in him all over again.

New Eyes

Anyone who has pastored for any length of time can become less caring and more clinical in their approach to people than they were at the beginning. We can get frustrated with those who seem to stay stuck in sin or brokenness. We can become quick to judge based on outward appearances and on assumptions. Of course, we don't call it judgment. We say we have become good

---

[6] Johnson, R. Skip. 2018. "Codependency and Codependent Relationships." BPD Family. Last modified May 16, 2019. https://bpdfamily.com/content/codependency-codependent-relationships.

judges of character, or that we can assess people well because of experience, or that we have discernment.

Through my experience of burnout, I have discovered that I may have no idea why someone behaves in a certain way. If I could not even explain my own behaviour to myself, how can I assume to fully understand someone else's? This understanding has created a new set of eyes in me. I am not nearly as quick to make assumptions about people. I have greater compassion and patience. This is not to say sin is excused, but rather I want to see the root of the sin destroyed, not just the behaviour altered. Jesus came not just to alter our behaviour but to change our hearts. More than ever, I am wanting to start with giving people the benefit of the doubt. God invites you to see him and others with a fresh set of eyes—the kind of eyes Jesus has when he looks at people.

Humility

We often joke around about the guy who wrote the book *The World's Ten Most Humble Men, And How I Trained the Other Nine* (not an actual book). I always considered myself reasonably humble, and others have often affirmed that in me. However, after discovering such frailty and weakness following a lifetime of ministry, I have been humbled more deeply.

Humility is not self-abasement. It is the realization of what you can and cannot do and what only God can do. It is recognizing how deeply you really do need God, in every area of your life. It is the discovery of total dependency. I appreciate more than ever the verse, "But by the grace of God I am what I am[7]."

I am still learning to distinguish the difference between humility and confidence. The two seem to be polar opposites, but they are supposed to coexist in our lives. Humility is not being weak. It is being strong in the Lord. Confidence is not in your ability or capacity. It is fully trusting in God's provision of grace and strength in your life. God wants to strip pride from your life and show his mighty strength by his grace expressed in your life.

Moving Forward

Whether you are in ministry as a pastor, a ministry leader, a leadership team member, or any other, it is my hope that this book has provided encouragement, insight, and wisdom. Pastors and churches need not be permanently damaged by the burnout of their leaders.

During my time of recovery, there were moments when we wondered how the church would come out at the other end. There was a period of financial challenge; there were a few people who chose to leave. However, predominantly people pulled together and served like never before. The leadership team (interim pastor and elders) pulled together and moved as one. People prayed and trusted God to get the church through, which he did! We saw restoration of finances and attendance at the end. Not all who left returned, but new ones came.

---

[7] 1 Corinthians 15:10, ESV

God is in the redeeming business. He is able to cause things to turn out for good. Burnout can be averted altogether if these principles are applied in advance. God can help you avoid unnecessary pain and stress. He can also redeem whatever situation you find yourself in.

Consider my story, along with the principles and information in this book, with much prayer. This is not a process to be taken lightly. With God's help, humble people, and wise counsel, healing and wholeness can be brought to all involved.

May the Lord direct your hearts into God's love and Christ's perseverance. (2 Thessalonians 3:5)

Online Resource

If you are interested in taking an assessment for burnout, compassion fatigue, or vicarious trauma, you can follow the link below for some great resources to provide tools that can help you move forward.

I am an affiliate with Hope Made Strong, an online support ministry for those that work in the helper professions (pastors, ministry leaders, nurses, counsellors, etc.).

The online courses provide a series of tools to walk you through some of the things I have shared in this book.

You can check out the website at https://hopemadestrong.org for general information. If you decide to use the resources please use this link: https://hopemadestrong.mykajabi.com/a/24454/Nmo2iWwR as it is tied to my affiliate account.

Printed in Great Britain
by Amazon